ALLIGATORS

BY SHANNON JADE

Apex is distributed by North Star Editions:
sales@northstareditions.com | 888-417-0195

Produced for Apex by Red Line Editorial.

Photographs ©: Shutterstock Images, cover, 1, 4–5, 7, 10–11, 13, 18, 19, 22–23, 26–27, 29; iStockphoto, 6, 8–9, 12, 14–15, 16–17, 20–21, 24–25

Library of Congress Control Number: 2022910561

ISBN
978-1-63738-439-8 (hardcover)
978-1-63738-466-4 (paperback)
978-1-63738-517-3 (ebook pdf)
978-1-63738-493-0 (hosted ebook)

Printed in the United States of America
Mankato, MN
012023

NOTE TO PARENTS AND EDUCATORS

Apex books are designed to build literacy skills in striving readers. Exciting, high-interest content attracts and holds readers' attention. The text is carefully leveled to allow students to achieve success quickly. Additional features, such as bolded glossary words for difficult terms, help build comprehension.

TABLE OF CONTENTS

CHAPTER 1

ALLIGATOR ATTACK!

An alligator floats in a river. Only its eyes and nostrils show above the water. The alligator holds very still. It waits for **prey**.

An alligator's bumpy skin makes it look like a floating log.

Alligators often shake prey to kill them or break them into pieces.

A large bird lands near the shore. The alligator leaps out of the water. Its powerful jaws snap. They grab the bird.

Alligators can leap up to 6 feet (2 m) out of the water.

The alligator swallows the
bird in one big gulp. Then it
slides back into the water.
It watches the shore. Soon, it
might spot another bird.

STRONG SWIMMERS

Alligators are great swimmers. They have webbed feet and strong tails. They can run fast on land, too. But they can't run for long. So, alligators usually hunt from the water.

Alligators can swim as fast as 20 miles per hour (32 km/h).

CHAPTER 2

SWAMPY HOMES

Alligators are large reptiles. They have thick, scaly skin. Some alligators can grow 11 feet (3 m) long.

Male alligators can weigh up to 1,000 pounds (454 kg).

Most American alligators live in Florida or Louisiana.

Alligators live in warm places with fresh water. Some alligators live near lakes and swamps. Others make their homes in slow-moving rivers.

TWO TYPES

There are two different types of alligators. American alligators live in the southeastern United States. Chinese alligators are smaller. They live in eastern China.

Chinese alligators are very rare. There may be fewer than 150 in the wild.

Like all reptiles, alligators are **cold-blooded**. To stay warm, they **bask** in the sun. Alligators also dig burrows. They rest in these holes when the weather is cold.

FAST FACT

In the wild, alligators usually live about 50 years.

Alligators rest in the sun to keep their bodies warm.

CHAPTER 3

HUNGRY GATORS

Alligators are fierce **predators**. They hunt many types of birds, fish, and small animals. Large alligators may even eat deer or bears.

Alligators eat small prey in one bite. Alligators pull larger prey underwater to kill them.

Alligators use their senses of sight, touch, and smell to find prey.

Alligators hunt mostly at night. Their eyes see well in the dark. An alligator also has a strong sense of smell. When it finds prey, it uses its teeth to grab the animal.

TONS OF TEETH

An alligator has up to 80 teeth. If teeth break or wear down, they can grow back. During its life, an alligator may go through around 3,000 teeth!

Each tooth in an alligator's mouth can grow back up to 50 times.

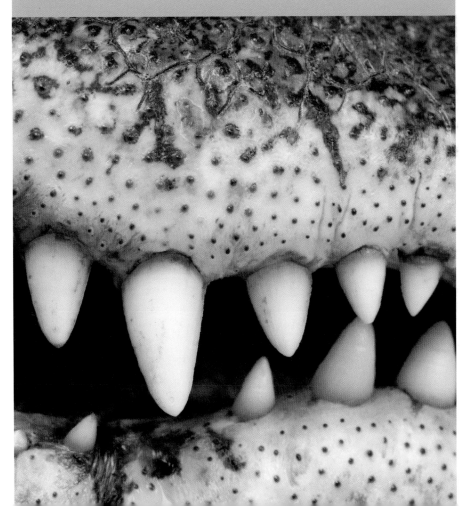

Sometimes alligators find and eat dead animals, including other alligators.

In addition to hunting, alligators can be **scavengers**. They eat whatever they can find. Some alligators even eat fruit.

FAST FACT

After meals, alligators can go a week without eating.

CHAPTER 4

LiFE iN THE WiLD

Most alligators live alone. But alligators may eat and bask in groups. Sometimes, they even hunt together.

Groups of alligators may gather in places with lots of food or sunlight.

Female alligators lay between 20 and 50 eggs at a time.

Alligators also come together to **mate**. Female alligators build nests on land. They lay eggs in the nests. After about 65 days, the eggs hatch.

FAST FACT

Male alligators tend to be larger than females.

The mother stays with her babies. She feeds and protects them. After one to three years, the young alligators are ready to live on their own.

Sometimes baby alligators ride on their mother's back.

GATOR DANGER

Adult alligators are high on the food chain. But baby alligators have many predators. Animals such as birds, raccoons, and larger alligators sometimes eat them.

COMPREHENSION QUESTIONS

Write your answers on a separate piece of paper.

1. Write a sentence describing where alligators live.

2. Would you like to see an alligator in the wild? Why or why not?

3. How many types of alligators are there?

    A. 2

    B. 4

    C. 6

4. How would a strong sense of smell help alligators hunt at night?

    A. They could get prey to come closer.

    B. They could find prey without swimming.

    C. They could find prey without needing to see it.

5. What does **powerful** mean in this book?

Its powerful jaws snap. They grab the bird.

    A. very strong

    B. very small

    C. very important

6. What does **burrows** mean in this book?

Alligators also dig burrows. They rest in these holes when the weather is cold.

    A. food animals catch and eat

    B. places animals stay away from

    C. homes animals make in the ground

Answer key on page 32.

GLOSSARY

bask
To lie in a warm place.

cold-blooded
Having a body temperature that matches the temperature of the surrounding water or air.

food chain
A list showing which animals eat others in a habitat.

mate
To form a pair and come together to have babies.

predators
Animals that hunt and eat other animals.

prey
Animals that are hunted and eaten by other animals.

reptiles
Cold-blooded animals that have scales.

scavengers
Animals that eat dead animals they did not kill.

TO LEARN MORE

BOOKS

Grack, Rachel. *Alligators*. Minneapolis: Bellwether Media, 2020.

Leaf, Christina. *Alligator or Crocodile?* Minneapolis: Bellwether Media, 2020.

Mattern, Joanne. *Alligators and Crocodiles*. Egremont, MA: Red Chair Press, 2018.

ONLINE RESOURCES

Visit **www.apexeditions.com** to find links and resources related to this title.

ABOUT THE AUTHOR

Shannon Jade writes both fiction and nonfiction books. She lives in Australia alongside some of the world's greatest landscapes and deadliest animals.

INDEX

ANSWER KEY:
1. Answers will vary; 2. Answers will vary; 3. A; 4. C; 5. A; 6. C